Mel Bay's First Lessons

Accordion

by Gary Dahl

3 4 5 6 7 8 9 0

It doesn't get any easier.....

Visit us on the Web at www.melbay.com — E-mail us at email@melbay.com

Contents

Foreword

This book is designed for the person who may know nothing about music and has had no previous piano accordion training.

Included with this book is an instructional recording that will motivate and guide the beginner student from basic accordion lessons to quickly playing enjoyable adult songs such as *Scarborough Fair* and *Ode to Joy*.

Goal summary for this book:

- Lesson pages that teach the basic necessary fundamentals of music for efficient, thrrorough progress.

- Reinforcement pieces that apply new concepts.

- No filler pages, i.e. maximum value per page.

- Theory pages that instill understanding and appreciation of music.

- Technique pages that develop good hand position, coordination, and finger independence.

- Interesting solo pieces that will inspire students to strive for higher levels of achievement.

- Instructional CD included to maximize motivation and comprehension

Enjoy the adventure!

Gary Dahl

Lesson 1
The *Accordion is a Free Reed Instrument

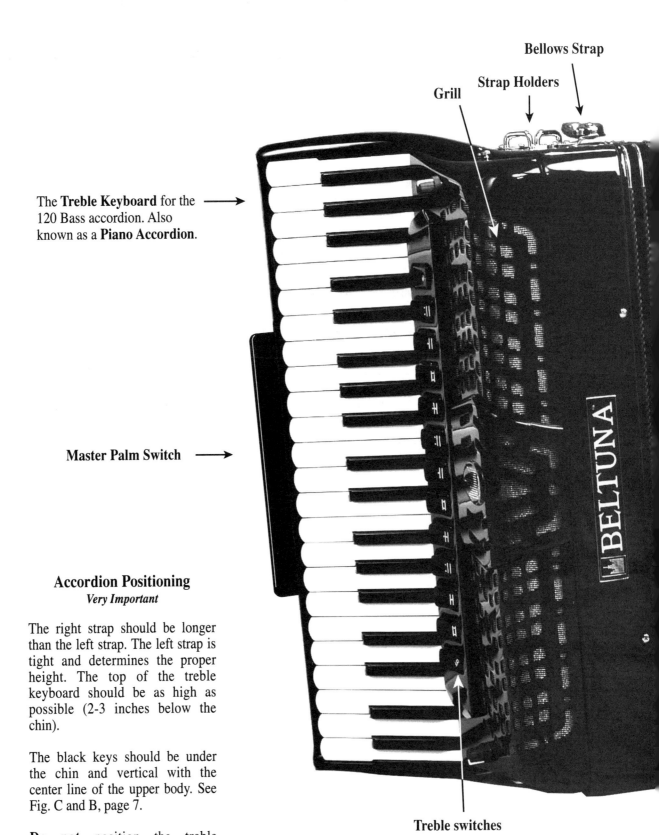

Bellows Strap

Strap Holders

Grill

The **Treble Keyboard** for the 120 Bass accordion. Also known as a **Piano Accordion**.

Master Palm Switch →

Treble switches

Accordion Positioning
Very Important

The right strap should be longer than the left strap. The left strap is tight and determines the proper height. The top of the treble keyboard should be as high as possible (2-3 inches below the chin).

The black keys should be under the chin and vertical with the center line of the upper body. See Fig. C and B, page 7.

Do not position the treble keyboard inside the right thigh. Keep knees as low as possible.

Pages 4 and 5 are loaded with basic information. Study and familiarize...

Refer to these pages as you progress through this book.

Bellows

Bass strap adjustment roller.

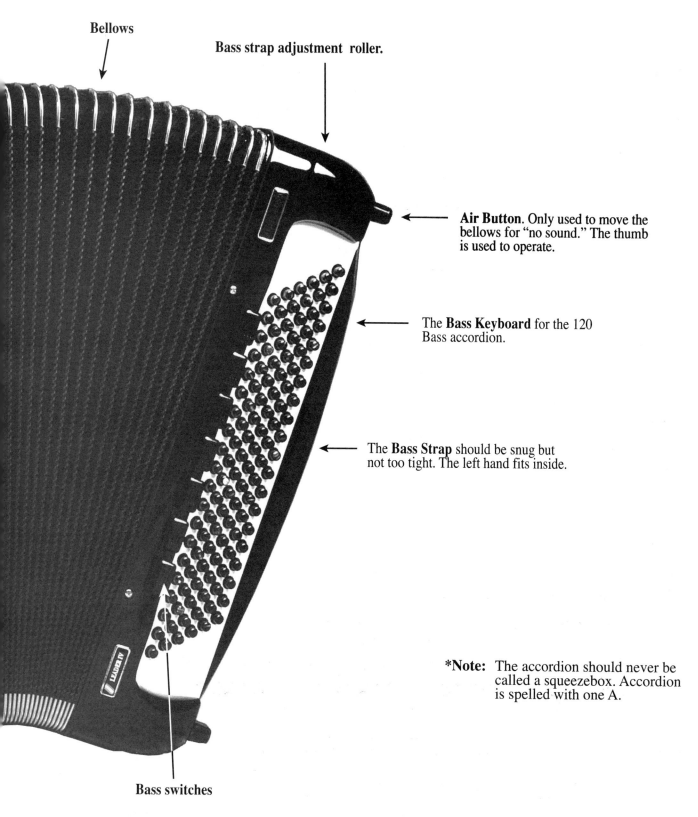

Air Button. Only used to move the bellows for "no sound." The thumb is used to operate.

The **Bass Keyboard** for the 120 Bass accordion.

The **Bass Strap** should be snug but not too tight. The left hand fits inside.

*Note: The accordion should never be called a squeezebox. Accordion is spelled with one A.

Bass switches

Unlock the **Bottom Bellows Strap** before putting on the accordion in sitting position.

Lesson 2
Basic Theory

This is a **Staff**. It has 5 lines and 4 spaces as numbered.

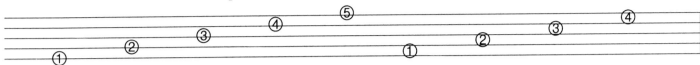

The notes (for corresponding keys and buttons) represent sound (tones)

This is a **Treble Clef Sign**. Adding this sign changes the name to **Treble Staff**.
The bottom line is always E. The bottom space is F.

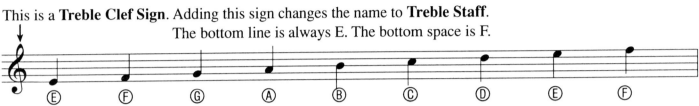

Music only has 7 letters in alphabetical order! (Note the alphabetical order)

Types of Notes

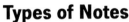

| Whole | Half | Dotted Half | Quarter | Eighth | Sixteenth |

Notation for more than one eighth note or sixteenth note = ♪♪ ← Beams → ♬

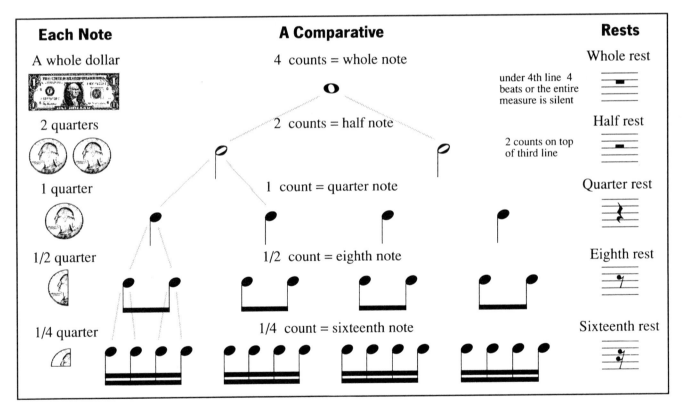

Each Note	**A Comparative**	**Rests**
A whole dollar	4 counts = whole note	Whole rest
		under 4th line 4 beats or the entire measure is silent
2 quarters	2 counts = half note	Half rest
1 quarter	1 count = quarter note	2 counts on top of third line
1/2 quarter	1/2 count = eighth note	Quarter rest
1/4 quarter	1/4 count = sixteenth note	Eighth rest
		Sixteenth rest

2 numbers at the beginning is a **Time Signature**. It officially tells us how to count time. The top number is *counts per measure*. The bottom 4 represents the quarter note, (as in 4 quarters in a dollar) and officially gives the quarter note one count.

Double bar line (End of Song)

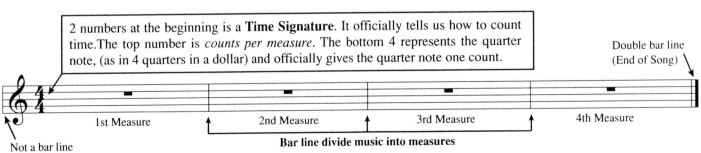

1st Measure   2nd Measure   3rd Measure   4th Measure

Not a bar line

Bar line divide music into measures

6

Lesson 3
Before We Begin Playing

Practice operating the bellows:

1. Place left hand inside the bass strap. Use air button and push bellows in to close completely and hold in until playing.

2. Press on the R.H. ⊖ (Bassoon) or ⊕ (Bandoneon) or ⊙⊙ (Violin) switch.

3. Place left hand in the approximate middle of the side bass panel after closing the bellows before starting to pull out.

Note: The bellows must be pulled (out) and pushed (in) smoothly, not in a jerky fashion. Pulling out will open the bellows more at the top (fan like). Keep the elbow close to your side. As you pull out the bellows will move downward a little automatically and to the back slightly. Don't worry, the bellows can bend. Simply retrace your steps upon pushing in. (Do **not** lift up your bellows while pushing in.)

4. Now you are ready to press down about 4 black keys in a group and hold them down to practice opening and closing the bellows smoothly until your music is pleasant to hear. Yes, you are playing music!

Note: The middle of the accordion (bottom of the bellows) will rest on top of the left thigh and the bellows will move to the left, outside and over the thigh. See Fig. C.

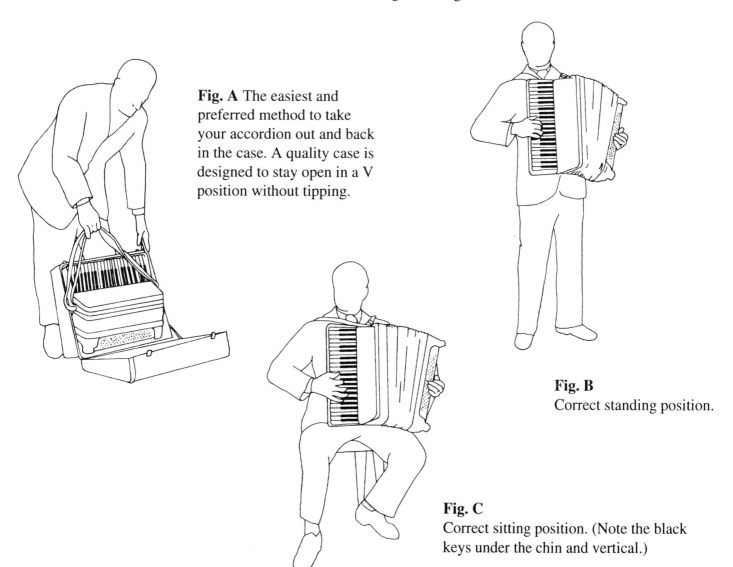

Fig. A The easiest and preferred method to take your accordion out and back in the case. A quality case is designed to stay open in a V position without tipping.

Fig. B
Correct standing position.

Fig. C
Correct sitting position. (Note the black keys under the chin and vertical.)

7

Lesson 4
Playing the Right Hand
and the Right Hand Position

Before playing our Right Hand (treble), we must discuss the right hand position.

1. Keep your thumb level and parallel to the white keys.

Example of parallel placement of thumb.

2. All other fingers should be slightly curved and close to the black keys, but <u>not</u> <u>inside</u> the black keys.

3. Keep your elbow out and back a little so your wrist is level and relaxed. (Remember, short fingernails)

Lesson 5
The Treble Keyboard
(Right Hand)

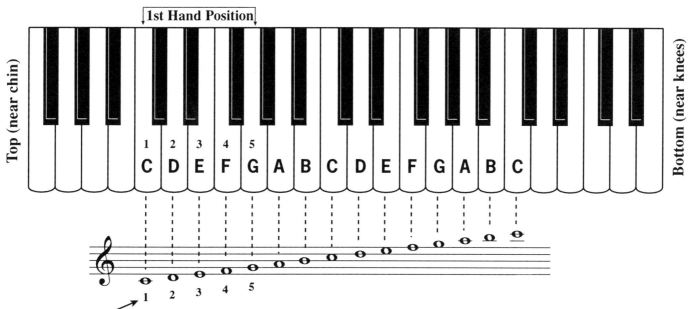

Fingers: 1=Thumb, 2=Index, 3=Middle, 4=Ring, 5=Small

Keep eyes on music while playing

(Quickly review page 7 before playing R.H.)

| Dotted half note: hold down 3 counts |

Medium volume

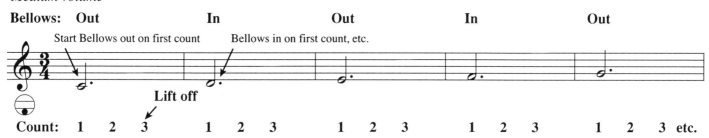

Count Out Loud Press and hold the key down on one and lift off on three.

Practice daily until played from start to end without stopping.
Always keep constant bellows pressure while playing.

Lesson 6
Playing the Left Hand

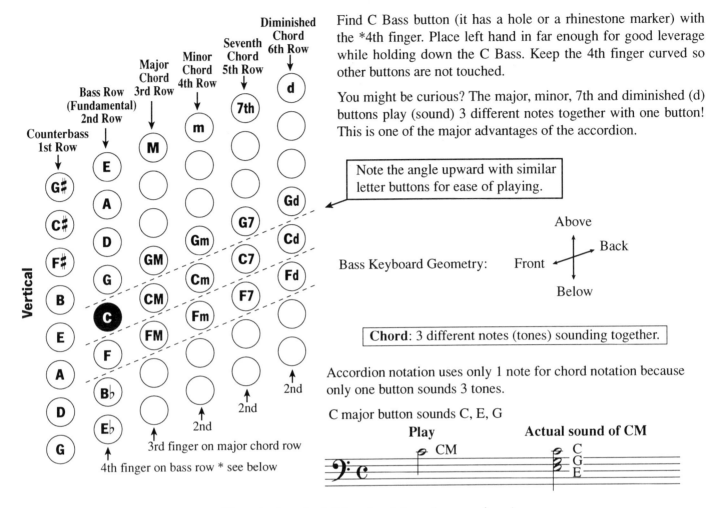

Find C Bass button (it has a hole or a rhinestone marker) with the *4th finger. Place left hand in far enough for good leverage while holding down the C Bass. Keep the 4th finger curved so other buttons are not touched.

You might be curious? The major, minor, 7th and diminished (d) buttons play (sound) 3 different notes together with one button! This is one of the major advantages of the accordion.

Note the angle upward with similar letter buttons for ease of playing.

Bass Keyboard Geometry: Above / Back / Front / Below

Chord: 3 different notes (tones) sounding together.

Accordion notation uses only 1 note for chord notation because only one button sounds 3 tones.

C major button sounds C, E, G

Play: CM   Actual sound of CM: C G E

(Never look at the left hand and **do not** use a mirror.)

This is a **Bass Clef Sign**. Play on the bass keyboard.

C ← C Bass is written on the 2nd space for the bass clef. Memorize the location on the bass staff for C, G, and F Bass notes.

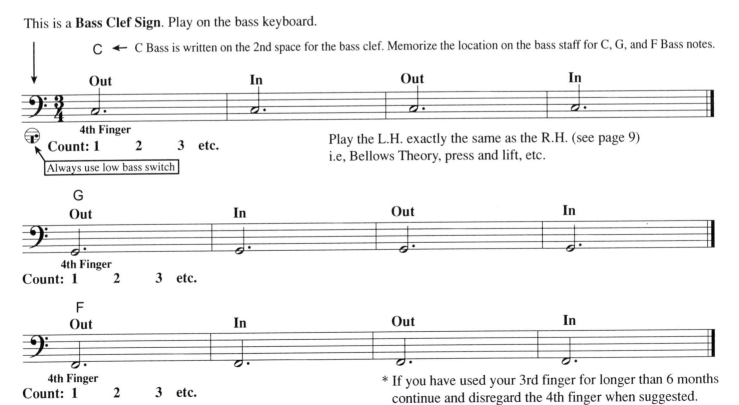

Play the L.H. exactly the same as the R.H. (see page 9) i.e, Bellows Theory, press and lift, etc.

* If you have used your 3rd finger for longer than 6 months continue and disregard the 4th finger when suggested.

Lesson 7

CM ← Only one M for Major chords is needed because this line contains only C Major chords.

Out   **In**   **Out**   **In**

3rd Finger

Count: 1   2   3   etc.

GM is the chord button directly above CM. Memorize CM, GM, and FM
GM ← locations (notes). All 3 have a clear and distinct appearance on music.

3rd

(Remember to practice all exercises many times daily)

Do not stop between measures

FM

3rd

This is a quarter note. Play very short (Bounce off... do not hold)

Play the notes even; similar to the beat of a clock second hand.

Out   **In**
C Bass   CM

4th   3rd

Play slowly...as in countling off seconds

Not necessary to count out loud now...

Remember bellows operation – Always maintain constant bellows pressure – There is still pressure between notes

Out   **In**
G Bass   GM

4   3

Out   **In**
F Bass   FM

4   3

Bass and chord practice   Now you have harmony and rhythm!

M

4   3   3 etc.

(It takes a pianist many years to achieve this!)

M

4   3   3 etc.

M

4   3   3 etc.

11

Lesson 8

𝄞 and 𝄢 Together

Beginning Coordination

Ready?

1. Start both hands at the same time (1st count).
2. Hold R.H. for 3 counts and lift off on 3rd count.

𝄽 Quarter Rest
one count of silence

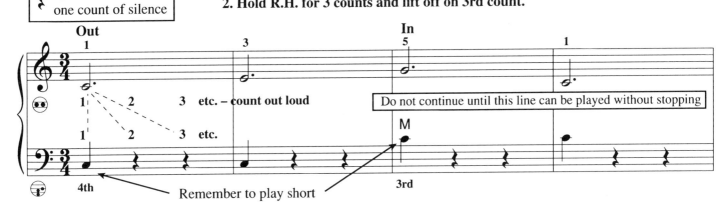

Do not continue until this line can be played without stopping

etc. – count out loud

Remember to play short

Lift off the right hand in the 3rd count of the L.H. chord

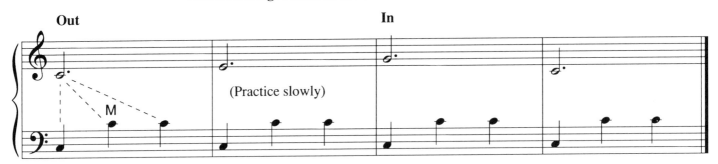

(Practice slowly)

Say the name of each note out loud (Review treble keyboard chart)

C   D   E   G   F   E   F   E   D   E   D   C

Random note selection (no melody)

♩ Quarter note = one count
play short; same as L.H.

Say the name of the note out loud while playing. Do not write names under each note.

Lesson 9

A Three Chord Song

(C Major, G Major, F Major)

Italian for moderately

Moderato (medium speed)

Only the starting finger is necessary to establish the hand position on the treble keyboard. At this time, use your note reading ability.

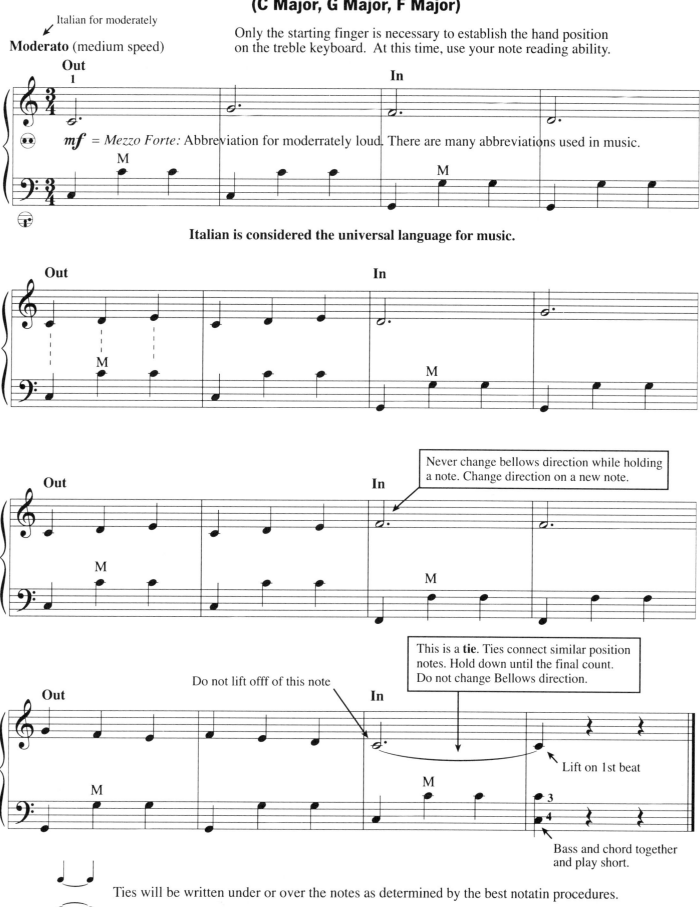

Italian is considered the universal language for music.

Never change bellows direction while holding a note. Change direction on a new note.

This is a **tie**. Ties connect similar position notes. Hold down until the final count. Do not change Bellows direction.

Do not lift offf of this note

Lift on 1st beat

Bass and chord together and play short.

Ties will be written under or over the notes as determined by the best notatin procedures.

13

Lesson 10
Learning More Treble Notes
(So we can play more interesting songs!)

Top (chin)

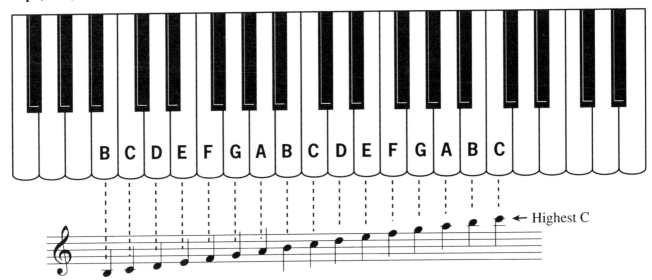

← Highest C

This isn't as hard as it looks....Just memorize. It will be simple after repetitive practice.

← The added short lines above and below the staff are **Ledger Lines**.

Why we need Ledger Lines is obvious.

4 counts per measure

Fingering is always logical...common sense

Cross 2nd finger over...very easy...Do Not play inside the black keys!

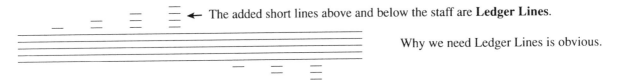

Very important: say each letter name out loud while playing each note. Do not write in letter names of each note.

Change fingers on the same key to raise our hand position.

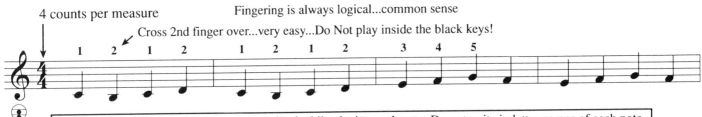

(You can't practice this note reading exercise too much!)

Play this exercise 2 ways: *short,* tap each key (note), and *legato,* hold down each note until the next note is played

More legato hints: strike each key....similar to a hammer hitting a nail.

Bring thumb up to B.
This will establish a new hand position

Lesson 11

Bass Solo Warm Ups

Adding D, A, B♭ and Minor Chords

Practice each line many times...4th finger only. We like to call the 4th finger the "Location Finger" because it is usually first to play

Memorize B♭, F, C, D, A Bass notes on the staff.

Minor practice

Note the angle upward to find minor... Hard to miss

Move straight down the railroad track to G...very easy

Bass and chord together

L. H. Exercise using 50's Rock Harmony

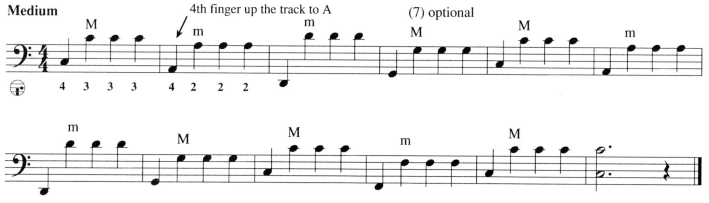

15

Lesson 12

Du, Du Liegst Mir Im Herzen

German Folk Song

Moderato — Start with 2nd finger — This is a **slur** (legato). Hold each note until the next note is played (see page 17)

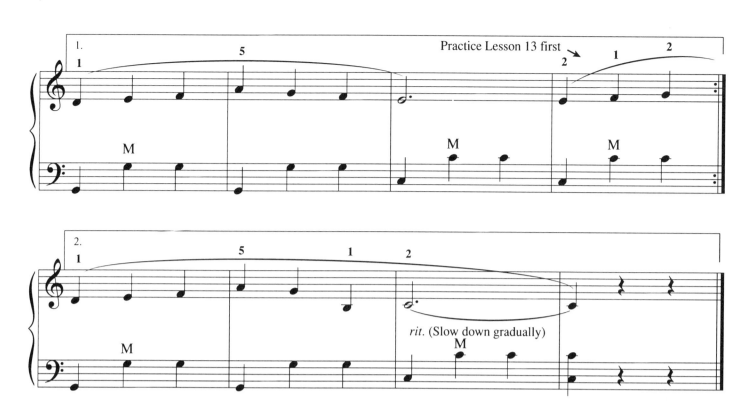

Slurs

*Slurs connect unlike positions   The **Slur**: hold the note until the next is played. Do not lift off before the next note is played.

> To Slur similar notes: hold note as long as possible and quickly move up and down for the next similar note on the proper beat. The finger will most likely not lift off the key. Learn to feel the spring loaded key.

First and Second Ending

Always repeat back to the nearest sign facing. Do this once.

1. (First time only)   2. (Second time only)

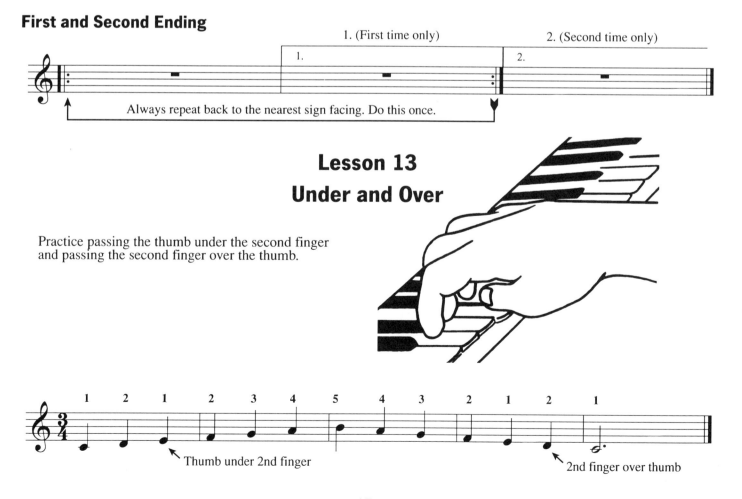

Lesson 13
Under and Over

Practice passing the thumb under the second finger and passing the second finger over the thumb.

Thumb under 2nd finger   2nd finger over thumb

(Lesson 13)
Waltz
from "Poet and Peasant"

Von Suppe

*rit. Abbreviation for **ritardando**, gradually slow tempo (rate of speed)

Abbreviation for **Da capo al fine**.
(Repeat from the beginning and end at *Fine*)

Lesson 14
The Village Tavern Polka
Introducing the L.H. 7th chord

Practice:

Repeat until on automatic!

L.H. in 4/4 time using the bass note on 1st and 3rd beat

Repetition will help you learn

Important! Remember: practice slowly enough for **NO** mistakes while in repetition.

Allegretto (lively, not too fast)

f *Forte* – loud

First four measures is the **Intro**

Remember: play all ♩ notes short.

Fingering is logical.

Do not write in letter names of notes

19

Lesson 15
Alternating the Basses

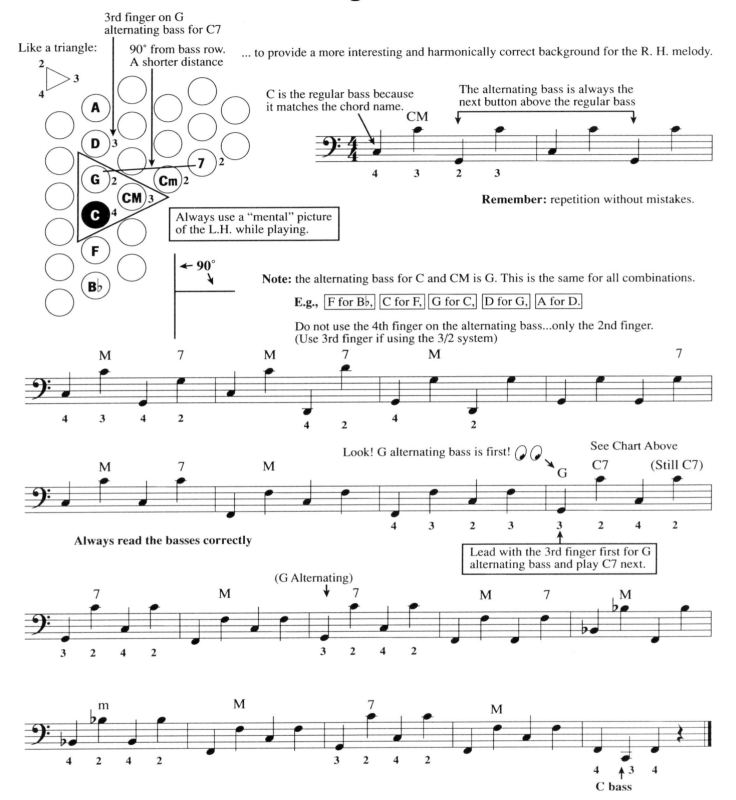

Lesson 16
The C Major Scale
(Review Page 17)

Practice at least 25 times daily

Practice staccato and legato. Start slowly and gradually increase speed.

Thumb under the 3rd finger

3rd finger over the thumb

Note: Make sure your 3rd finger is fairly close to the black keys when crossing over.
(Tip of the thumb remains in approx. center of white keys) (see pg. 8)

The Can Can
(From Orpheus in the Underworld)

Allegro (fast)

<u>B</u> counterbass is in front of G. (see pg. 27)

Offenbach

C Scale descending

Repeat as desired

21

Lesson 17

The L.H. Blues
(also used for rock and roll)

Just slightly hold each bass and chord together but do not connect.   Guitar style rhythm

Also known as "12 Bar Blues"

Hold sign – double or
more than 2 counts

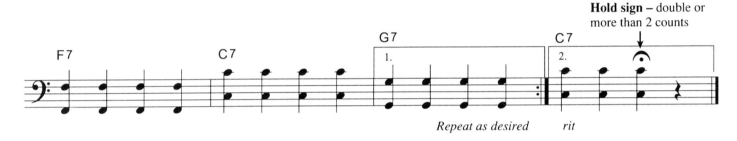

Repeat as desired   rit

If you want to improvise the R.H. while playing the L.H., use only these notes, in any random order you choose.
Listen to CD track #17 for ideas.

A flat (f) lowers a note one-half step, or one key on the deyboard.
For example, Bf is the black key to the left of B natural.

(Only use C with F7)
(Only use G with G7)

22

Lesson 18

Goodnight Ladies
(Now for a little fun...a few practice songs)

Allegretto

Traditional

23

Lesson 19
Scarborough Fair

Andante (Slowly but moving)

Old Traditional

2nd time - try the ⊖ switch and play 8va

Fermata (hold sign) - hold longer than 3 counts

rit.

Repeat as desired

* Abbreviation for *ritardando* (gradually slower).

Lesson 20

Tiritomba

(Practice page 26 first)

Italian Folksong

Allegretto   (All ♩ Notes Staccato)

Cont. next page

> The **accent:** apply a quick jerk with the bellows at the start of the note

Playing 2 notes at the same time
This is really very easy

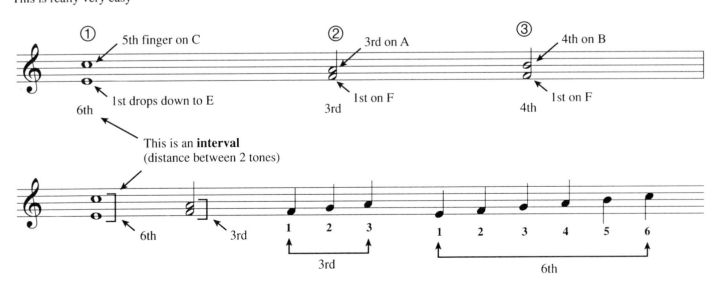

Lesson 21

Aloha Oe
Introducing the Counterbass with the Extended 4th Finger

Lesson 22
Introducing Eighth Notes
And Counting Theory

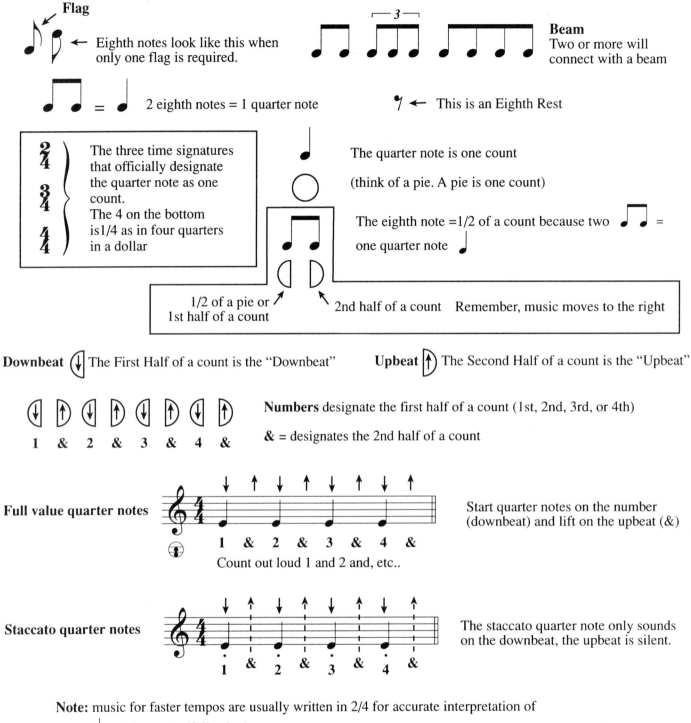

Flag ← Eighth notes look like this when only one flag is required.

Beam Two or more will connect with a beam

2 eighth notes = 1 quarter note

↖ This is an Eighth Rest

The three time signatures that officially designate the quarter note as one count.
The 4 on the bottom is 1/4 as in four quarters in a dollar

The quarter note is one count

(think of a pie. A pie is one count)

The eighth note = 1/2 of a count because two = one quarter note

1/2 of a pie or 1st half of a count

2nd half of a count   Remember, music moves to the right

Downbeat The First Half of a count is the "Downbeat"

Upbeat The Second Half of a count is the "Upbeat"

1 & 2 & 3 & 4 &

Numbers designate the first half of a count (1st, 2nd, 3rd, or 4th)

& = designates the 2nd half of a count

Full value quarter notes

1 & 2 & 3 & 4 &
Count out loud 1 and 2 and, etc..

Start quarter notes on the number (downbeat) and lift on the upbeat (&)

Staccato quarter notes

1 & 2 & 3 & 4 &

The staccato quarter note only sounds on the downbeat, the upbeat is silent.

Note: music for faster tempos are usually written in 2/4 for accurate interpretation of ♩ quarter notes (full value).

A faster moving piece (tempo) written in 4/4 will automatically be played with staccato quarter notes unless a slur is written.

Upbeats are silent

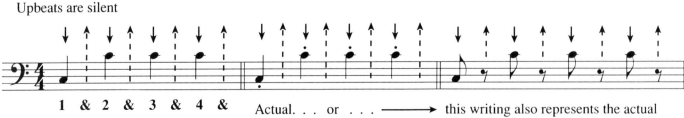

1 & 2 & 3 & 4 &
Correct Bass and Chord accompaniment is automatically played Staccato (short)

Actual. . . or . . . → this writing also represents the actual playing but is too cluttered.

28

Lesson 23

Exercises

Slowly at first, then play at faster tempos.
Repeat many times daily

Remember: The downbeats (1, 2, 3, 4) must be steady and even.

1 & 2 & 3 & 4 &   1 & 2 & 3 & 4 &   1 & 2 & 3 & 4 &

Count when playing slowly .... not possible at faster tempos

The Same Exercise, Both Hands

Lesson 24

Jingle Bells

Lesson 25
The Dotted Quarter Note

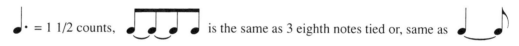

Remember, the left hand doesn't sound on the upbeat ↑

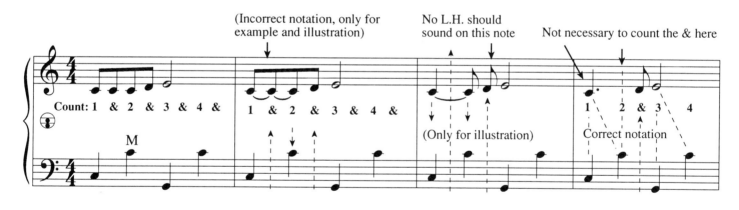

Remember to lift

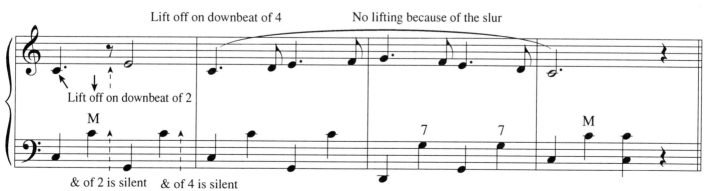

31

Lesson 26

Ode to joy

Andante

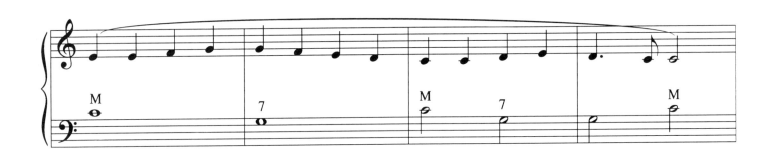

M (chord only style)

⊕ Use tenor switch if you have it   (Keep your 4th finger on bass row for location)

rit.